EVERYTHING YOU NEED TO KNOW ABOUT THE INCUBUS DEMON

Spirit Husband and Spirit Wife, Incubus and Succubus Demons, Marine Spirits, All Sex Demons

REV. EZEKIEL KING

Copyright 2020 @ Rev. Ezekiel King

Disclaimer: This book contains images, extracts, and quotations from the Holy Bible, famous figures of the past, and a few reliable online sources. As such, credits have been given where due.

All other information contained herein is either that of the author or extracts from his other books.

MORE BOOKS BY THE AUTHOR

Listed below are some other books by this author available on Amazon. To find a full collection of them and more, please visit our website:

Christianvy.com
The Christian Victory Year

- **Total Deliverance from Spirit Husband and Spirit Wife, Incubus and Succubus Demons:** *Incubus Demon and All Sex Demons of the Night*

- **Unmasking and Defeating Demons:** *150 Questions and Answers About Demons and Evil*

Spirits (Demon Attack, Spiritual Warfare, Demonic Possession, Demonic Covenants and Curses, Demonic Deliverance)

- **How to Pray to God and Always Be Heard:** *The Power of Prayers Done Right*

- **19 True Incubus Short Stories:** *Incubus and Succubus True Stories, Spirit Husband and Spirit Wife Stories, Marine Spirit Spouses Stories, Ghost Sex Demons Stories – The Reality*

- **Spiritual Marriage, Women, Pregnancy, And Childbirth:** *Physical and Spiritual Warfare Against Spiritual Husband, Incubus Demon and Marine Spirits (All Sex Demons)*

There is also a comprehensive ***Deliverance Series*** for you. Check out our website... **Christianvy.com**

FOREWORD

The information contained in this book is entirely true and accurate facts of life and spirituality. No aspect of it may be regarded as fiction or fabrication, and as such, may be acted upon accordingly.

DEDICATION

7

This book is dedicated to my God and my calling to his work.

TABLE OF CONTENT

INTRODUCTION

For our struggle is not against flesh and blood, but against the rulers, against the powers, against the world forces of this darkness, against the spiritual forces of wickedness in the heavenly places.

- Ephesians 6:12

Most people do not believe in the existence of demons, supernatural creatures of utter evil whose primary goal is to exploit and destroy humanity. We live in ignorance, and yet these invisible evil creatures are present and very active among us.

There is a particular group of demons that specialize in using sex as a weapon against humans. They are powerful, intelligent, and knowledgeable creatures. They vary in kind, and so do their methods of attack.

The sex is always fantastic, better than normal. It happens spiritually, in dreams, but the feeling is always physically. We forget it because it's a dream, nothing more. Time passes, more episodes occur and we ignore them. Soon we forget and stop noticing them. When the terrible consequences finally set in, we fail to make the connection to the origin.

... Okay, so last night, I had a pretty bizarre, meandering dream. The part that really stands out to me was I was in a dark place and there was some kind of ritual going on. These two people threw me down into a coffin that was in an open grave and then something had me by the waist and raped me. I

13

actually woke up having an orgasm. While drifting back to sleep, I kept hearing this voice saying things like 'I've loved you from afar for so long, I adore you, just let me love you please.'. It was a male voice, and he said it over and over and over again, just begging me. I kept getting flooded with warm and fuzzy, lovey-dovey images.

While this was happening, I heard another voice say, 'don't fall for it. It will use whatever means it can think of to try and get you to consent. It will lie to you, it will guilt you, it will imitate past lovers to get to *you. Just tell it to go away'. So with a great deal of struggle, I was able to tell it to go away.*

So strange. I'm not sure what brought this on, but last night, there was a storm, and our power went out. Everything in the house felt really strange and unsettling for a little while. I'm used to storms where I live but there was something sketchy going on last night for sure. Anyway, what are your thoughts? Is it something I should be concerned about returning? Should I do something like burn Sage or make a Sigil for protection? This is kind of out of the left field for me

These vile creatures...what are they? Where do they come from? How do they enter one's life? How do they operate, and how do we defeat or stop them?

You'll learn most of what you need to know in the following chapters, and it'll shock you.

THE REALITY

The name ***Incubus Demon*** is commonly used in reference to a large group of very ancient evil supernatural creatures that have been on earth for millions of years. They first arrived sometime after the creation of the earth and its subsequent destruction by the great floods.

From that early period on, even until today, their primary objective has been to have sex with humans in one way or the other. Hence, they are also referred to as ***sex demons***.

Different Methods of Attack, One Weapon

There are different kinds of *sex demons* with different powers and abilities, which defines their attack method.

The attacks of a *sex demon* may get very complicated, but, in one way or the other, (immoral) sex is always involved. That is how you know them.

INCUBUS AND SUCCUBUS DEMON

Based on their activities among humans, *sex demons* appear to have both male and female versions. The male version remains known as an *Incubus demon*, while the female version is better known as a *Succubus demon*.

What Is an Incubus?

An Incubus is a male demon (or spirit) that preys on women, particularly while they are asleep. They attack, rape, and sometimes impregnate their victims.

The woman may awaken while being raped or may not even know anything has occurred until her health suddenly begins to deteriorate as she hosts the growing parasitic baby of the *Incubus demon*.

What Is a Succubus?

A succubus is a female *Incubus demon* (spirit) that preys on men, especially while they are asleep. A Succubus demon will often get pregnant for a man, and the result is a spiritual child.

According to their evil nature, both the spirit mother and child will wreak havoc in the man's life.

Difference Between Incubus and Succubus Demons?

The difference between the *Incubus and Succubus demons* lies solely in gender, which defines their operation mode. The *Succubus demon* attacks men only, while the *Incubus demon* preys exclusively on women.

21

SPIRIT HUSBAND AND SPIRIT WIFE

An *Incubus Demon* can become permanently attached to or fixated on a victim. When this occurs, a strong bond similar to marriage is formed. Such bonds are typically called **spiritual marriage,** and the attacking demon is referred to as a ***spirit husband*** or ***spirit wife***.

Spirit Husband

An *Incubus demon* that has become permanently attached to a female victim (woman) is referred to as a ***spirit husband***.

Spirit Wife

A *Succubus demon* that becomes attached to a male victim (man) is referred to as a ***spirit wife***.

Spirit Spouses

In that way people commonly refer to their legal husbands and wives as spouses, so they also refer to spirit husbands and spirit wives as spirit spouses.

Spiritualists are often guilty of this.

Spirit Children

Spirit or spiritual children are the products of spiritual marriages and can be spiritual or physical.

MARINE SPIRITS

Marine spirits are the worst kinds of *sex demons*. They are very powerful and incredibly resilient. The problems they bring are so terrible and complicated that deliverance is often tricky. These creatures fully possess their victims' lives, enslave, and use them against other humans.

10 WEIRD FACTS ABOUT INCUBUS DEMON

Here are some weird facts about the **Incubus demon** that'll shock you in no small way.

1. Incubus and Succubus History is Ancient

People have recognized the existence of the **Incubus and Succubus demons** since as far back as the ancient Mesopotamian civilization in 2500 BCE, the earliest civilization on earth, which is mentioned several times in the Holy Bible.

The **Incubus demon** also appears in the earliest work of fiction in existence, **The Epic of Gilgamesh**. In it, Gilgamesh's father is portrayed as a demon who attacks and rapes sleeping women.

2. Incubus Names Are Numerous

The ***Incubus and Succubus demons***
have been known by so many names over the
ages. Top on that list is ***spirit husband and
Spirit wife***, ***Incubi and Succubi*** (Latin),
Incubo and Succubo (old Latin), ***Lilu*** *and*
Lilitu, demons of lust, demons of the night, and
finally, sex demons.

3. The Meaning of Incubus Lies in Ancient History

In ancient Mesopotamia, these *sex
demons* were known as ***Lilu*** and ***Lilitu***. With
time, Latin became the official language of the
civilized world, and the names of these demons
changed.

Lilu became ***Incubo*** or ***Incubi***, which
means *"a nightmare induced by such a demon"*,
while the female version ***Lilitu*** became known
as ***Succubi***

When translated directly from Latin to English, **Incubi** and **Succubi** become **Incubus** and **Succubus**.

4. Incubus Bonds Lead to Death

Since these *sex demons* often become fixated on a particular victim (forming a bond of spiritual marriage), some women have been known to die from exhaustion after repeated visits by the same *Incubus demon*.

5. Incubus Sleep Paralysis Are real

Incubus demons have been known to put their victims into a deep trance-like state during attacks so that they cannot move or call out for help. **Sleep paralysis** is how medical experts explain away this strange phenomenon.

6. Incubus Attacks Lead to Terrible Misfortunes

Incubus demon attacks lead to terrible misfortunes in life such as sickness, financial losses, problems in marriage and relationships, mental issues, etc., even death.

7. Incubus Attacks Can Last for Generations

It's not just the attacks of the *Incubus demon* but the consequences too. They can actually continue from one generation to the other.

8. Incubus Demons Can Bond with Babies

Yes, the *Incubus Demon* can bond with little babies, even those not yet born or still in their mother's womb.

9. Incubus Victims Abound (You're not alone)

One study showed that as many as 12% of people experience Incubus attacks in their lifetime. However, that study characterized the phenomena as a bizarre form of sleep paralysis.

10. Variations of The Incubus Demon Abound

Because of the Incubus demons' widespread activities throughout human history on earth, people of different lands and clime traditionally have different variations of this particular demon wrapped in layers of myths and legends. We've already talked about some of them and will look at more in the next chapter.

29

VARIATIONS OF THE INCUBUS DEMON AROUND THE WORLD

Folklore, Myths, and Legends about the *Incubus demon* abound from different parts of the world. We take a look at just a few here.

The Incubus demon is worshipped in some lands.

1. Chilean Folklore

The ***Trauco***, in Chile, is a small, ugly, human-like creature who attacks and attracts women. This entity's activities are believed not

31

to be restricted to night time alone, and a lot of unexplainable pregnancies are credited to it.

2. German Folklore

The ***Alp*** is a vampire-like creature believed to visit its victims mainly at night. This creature possesses magical powers and wears a cape called a ***Tarnkappe***.

3. South African Folklore

The ***Popobawa*** in southern Africa is a shape-shifting evil demon who stalks women at night from the shadows and rapes them. The only way to stop the repeated attacks of a ***Popobawa*** is by telling other people about it (sounds a lot like a Christian confessional, doesn't it?).

4. Norse Folklore

A ***Mare*** is a small demonic being that sits on the chest of a sleeping person, inducing nightmares (see the image at the top of this article).

5. Western Christianity

Renowned Christian theologian St. Thomas Aquinas (1225 –1274) believed in the existence of the *Incubus demon*, saying, "*Still, if some are occasionally begotten from demons, it is not from the seed of such demons, nor from their assumed bodies, but from the seed of men, taken for the purpose; as when the demon assumes first the form of a woman, and afterward of a man; just so they take the seed of other things for other generating purposes.*"

His theory was a bit bizarre, but the suspicion was there.

6. The Incubus Demon in American Pop Culture

Over the years, Hollywood has produced several movies centered around true-life stories of the *Incubus demon,* and some of the best known are **Incubus** (1966), **The Incubus** (1982), and, last, **Incubus** (2006).

You'll often find these movies portraying the *Incubus demon* as some kind of blood-sucking vampire creatures that also has sex with its victims. What you have to understand about Hollywood is that it's not always about the truth but about profit – the movies are modified to captivate viewers' attention.

ARE INCUBUS AND SUCCUBUS THE SAME AS VAMPIRES?

People often ask, 'What Is the Difference Between a Vampire and an *Incubus Demon*?'

Answer... The *Incubus demon* and the creatures known as Vampires are similar enough to be confused as one and the same by many people but are not.

The difference between a vampire and an *Incubus demon* is that a vampire is the Hollywood version of a dead human 'coming back to life' due to some evil ritual or the other. On the other hand, an *Incubus* is a supernatural entity that is not and was never human.

DO INCUBUS AND SUCCUBUS REALLY EXIST?

The *Incubus and Succubus demons* are creatures of sexual perversion that take advantage of human weakness. Do not take these demons lightly or the topic as unreal. If you are a person that feels that demons do not exist, then answer just one simple question…

Have you ever had intercourse in a dream and actually felt like it really took place? You even climax in reality. If the answer is *yes*, then you have been a victim of one of these demons.

> *The greatest trick*
> *Satan ever played on man*
> *is to convince him that he*
> *does not exist!*

Night demons (*Incubus and Succubus demons*) are very real, and they are beings of lust. They are very powerful, high-ranking demons in the world of evil, and their activities have been observed by humans for thousands of years.

Perhaps you wonder how it is even possible for spiritual beings to have any manner of sexual intercourse with humans. The answer is complicated and explained at length in my book ***Total Deliverance from Spirit Husband and Spirit Wife,*** but you can take my word here. It is all too easy for powerful supernatural beings to have sexual intercourse with humans - do not forget now that demons are merely fallen angels. The question here should be; can angels interact directly with humans in any way? The next chapter answers this question.

Can Angels Take on Human Form?

All through the Bible, there are many references and evidence of supernatural beings of high order taking on some type of physical form and functioning correctly as such.

In the opening chapters of the Book of Genesis, for example, the start of chapter 6, in particular, tells of Angels taking human form.

"And when men began to multiply upon the earth, they had daughters, 2. The angels saw these daughters of men that they were beautiful, and they chose and took wives of them."
-Genesis 6: 1-2

Simply put, supernatural beings came down from Heaven and had sex with beautiful 'human' women.

Satan, who is a spirit, a fallen angel, in fact, took on the physical form of a snake (serpent) to tempt Eve. A process that entailed his speaking to her (Rev 12:9, Gen 3:1-5).

There is even some mention of God and some angels also taking on physical forms and function as human beings. Go read through the book of Genesis, begin from chapter 18 and on to chapter 19, through to verses 23 (Genesis 18-19:25 - Use the New Living Translation Bible for better understanding), and you will find all the proof you need.

In the text, the living God and two angels manifested themselves as human beings and functioned as such in a visit to Abraham on route to destroy the twin cities of Sodom and Gomorrah.

They actually speak, eat, walk, rest, sleep, and even have their feet washed. This is proof apparent that spirits of a high order can indeed manifest themselves in physical form.

Going further through the scriptures, other references to this point are to be found as well. So there is no need to be mystified by the prospect of spirits taking on human form. However, if you have to be mystified or even doubt that these evil demons of the night exist, then consider this point...

Ever heard of **Saint Augustine**? According to Wikipedia, he was one of the first saints of the Christian church to bring to light the secret activities of certain spirits that specialized in sleeping with human beings, particularly women, in abusive ways.

In his day, they called these spirits **Incubo** (meaning nightmare), and soon, it became the custom that women who got pregnant right after such experiences were burned alive at the stake.

Yes, indeed, **sex demons** do exist. The encounters that people share today about sex demons (having serious phenomenal sex in dreams) are actual experiences and not schizophrenic episodes, which is how highly trained doctors (shrinks) try to de-validate these strange occurrences.

ARE WE REALLY BEING ATTACKED?

Whether or not a person is really being attacked by these demons is usually pretty obvious. The evil beings manifest themselves in full to your conscious mind and, in the process, cause you to experience all the stimulations and physical sensations that take place during actual sexual intercourse or sexual contact with a normal physical person.

Sometimes people are so mystified by the activities of these evil spirits that they find it difficult believing any of it is real. They wonder if the demons even exist!

In very severe situations, these demons reveal themselves clearly to their victims during night-time hours and sometimes, even during the day. There have been many reports with people claiming to have actually seen spiritual beings with physical abilities that come and subject them to various kinds of sexual acts and abuse.

These spiritual beings are often violent and can attack you – choking, beating, and restraining you. They sometimes even disturb things around you, even break certain objects in your home.

HOW TO KNOW IF YOU ARE HAVING INCUBUS ATTACKS

Battling Sexual Urges and Masturbation

One of the major effects of these spirits on people is inducing overwhelming sexual urges in their bodies.

This is one of the easiest ways to discover if you are being attacked by these vile demons. The sexual urges brewing within you is so strong that they completely take over your entire mind.

This can occur at any time of the day, but it happens mostly when you are lying down all alone. You simply cannot think of anything else at that point in time, and it seems like nothing you try or do to make the urges go away works (i.e., take a cold shower, force yourself into another activity, shift position to another place.).

It would appear that the only relief from the terrible urge is to have an orgasm by any means whatever. Most often than not, you will have the orgasm spontaneously, and they'll turn out to be unusually strong, better than normal.

If you have this kind of urges, THEY ARE BY NO MEANS NORMAL!

Note, I'm not saying that every powerful sexual urge that hits the body is caused by demonic manifestations of one form or the other. Not at all. Strong sexual urges can be very normal, purely hormonal, or just plain old-fashioned arousal at the thought of having a good time with your partner.

However, when sexual urges come on too suddenly, without reason or warning. Coming on at very inappropriate times, without any external stimulations whatever, and you simply cannot bring them under control without an intense battle within yourself, that is when you know you are being attacked by a sex demon.

In this situation, you act blindly, without thought of the consequence. Sexual release is what you want at all costs, and after that, there is only a deep sense of regret.

Sorry to tell you, but you have been used and dumped by a sex demon, and they're most likely not done with you.

WHAT ARE INCUBUS DREAMS?

Incubus Dreams are dreams induced by the *Incubus demon* (or Succubus demon). They are compelling experiences and count as one way of knowing if you're a victim of these demons.

Incubus Dreams can be divided into two categories: sex dreams and nightmares.

Sex Dreams

These are dreams in which you become engaged in spectacular sexual acts that have your body undergoing spontaneous orgasms like never before.

Nightmares

Another less obvious manifestation of these demons is in the induction of nightmares – realistic, even graphic, heart-stopping nightmares that jerk you out of sleep, take the sleep from you completely, and leave you frightened.

THE ULTIMATE PURPOSE OF THE INCUBUS DEMON?

As with all demons, the ultimate purpose of the *Incubus and Succubus demons* is the destruction of humanity. This they go about achieving in different complex ways.

According to Genesis 6, the purpose of these demons of the night is to impregnate (fill) you with evil, and nothing good comes from such a thing...

"4 In those early days, giants lived on earth because whenever the angels had intercourse with the daughters of men, they bore children who became giants."

The scripture gives us to understand that when these demons (fallen angels) had sex with the lovely women of the world, these women got pregnant and gave birth to abnormal children... abominations – utter perversions of nature -- wicked giants.

The *Incubus and Succubus demons* are chief demons that fall right into this class of fallen angels that operated in those early times. The difference here is that they are now looking to impregnate (or fill) YOU with the spiritual perversion of nature.

Once these spirits have you trapped by sexually aroused or subdue you through violence, you become so weak, your defenses are down, and your conscious guard is non-existent. They can then manipulate your subconscious mind in a way that will go unnoticed for such a long time as they do you significant damage spiritually.

This situation is quite similar to how a woman surrenders herself completely to the enjoyment of intercourse with a man and allows him to plant deeply within her all that comes out of him.

On the other hand, it is also the way a girl who is being molested is subjected to the control of the molester. Once this seed is planted inside, the woman does not know what it does or where it goes, but it would definitely change her in significant ways. She may have contracted an STD or even conceived, sometimes both, but this she will not be aware of for quite a while.

In that way your natural body is weak and tired (fatigued) after normal intercourse with a real partner, so also will an encounter with an Incubus or Succubus demon leave you feeling spiritually and emotionally drained, usually because they steal a lot of things from you, including spiritual strength, purity of soul, and virtue.

In place of what they have stolen, they impregnate (fill) you with their evil seeds of perversion and lust.

Like an abusive partner or a rapist, these spirits will attempt to bring you under their control, subdue you and make you feel worthless.

Although these demons are so skilled at inducing extreme sexual pleasures, they make a person feel miserable in every other way. The ecstasy and complete fulfillment that you experience with these spirits sexually are always exceedingly more intense than natural sex, so it is highly addictive. You will do anything to get it. This has the psychological effect of inducing guilt, lowering your resistance even more.

The aim of the nightmares is to plant deep within you the element of fear, therefore limiting your faith in deliverance. The idea behind this is that put up fear brings about a desire to seek out an outlet of release or comfort.

Sexual activity, particularly masturbation and sexual fantasy, bring about a temporary sense of release and comfort. Therefore, by inducing the fear in their victims, these lustful demons ensure you stay hooked to sexually perverse acts as a means of release.

A more important consequence of this fear is that it robs Christians of faith and the willingness to present themselves before God. This perversion of your faith, the fear, and the shame you feel mean that your entire relationship with God and the ultimate purpose for your life has been effectively undermined.

Without faith, what can Christians accomplish? Nothing. In our subconscious state of perversion, nothing is possible, particularly a connection with God.

People that are hit by Incubus and Succubus, these terrible and very clever sex demons of the night, will experience a considerable amount of failure in life and may even end up feeling "cursed" with bad luck. For Christians, there is no such thing as being cursed with bad luck in this situation – your entire belief system has been effectively perverted!

WHERE DOES THE INCUBUS DEMON COME FROM?

As mentioned repeatedly, these demons are actually fallen angels. Yes, they were once angels who lived and worship in Heaven, that most holy place.

The Bible teaches us that in the day the angels of Heaven saw the beauty of the daughters of man and came down to the earth to 'take themselves wives' among them, it so displeased God that he did two things, one of which was to shut those angels of Heaven forever.

So, where do the Succubus and Incubus demons come from? These vile sex demons that rule the night? They came from Heaven millions of years ago, thrown out of their original abode!

THE POWER OF THE INCUBUS DEMON IN YOUR LIFE

The power of the *Incubus demon* at work in a victim's life is mostly based on lust – the lust for sex.

Lust

Lust is a deep-set desire for illegal pleasure. Nothing good comes of such things.

In lust is a willingness to meet a very natural and legal need or desire in a sinful or illicit manner.

For example, it is necessary for every human being to eat food; but to fulfill that same need through gluttony (overfeeding or overeating) is lust. To desire nice things is very natural, but the willingness to meet that desire through trickery and dishonesty means is lust.

There is really nothing sinful about a human being's natural, God-given sexual urges, but to fulfill those particular urges through sexual perversion and/or masturbation is lust.

Bottom line – LUST IS A HUGE SIN – and sin is something that God, an utterly Holy being, does not welcome in any manner.

As long as these spirits can afflict your body, there is an open door of sin in your life.

HOW TO DEFEAT INCUBUS AND SUCCUBUS INDUCED LUST

Accepting accountability is the first step to deliverance. In the case of these tricky night demons, accept that you are at fault for not being in your rightful place of authority over them and allowing them to control your actions to the extent of running riot in your life.

Go to work, examine your lifestyle and your heart in the light of God's truth to find that open door. Once you find it, slam that door shut for good and be free. Enjoy the freedom of Jesus Christ!!!

Activities Fueled by Lust

Below is a list of activities fueled by lust, the number one weapon of the *Incubus and Succubus demons.*

1. Fornication: Incest, adultery, homosexuality, etc.
2. Masturbation
3. Pornography Addiction
4. Carnality: Spending a lot of time on non-spiritual activities
5. Bitterness and Unforgiveness
6. Fear and Doubt: The undoing of every Christian
7. Witchcraft
8. Abuse: You are the victim of the abusive demons
9. Molestation
10. Emotional Wounds
11. Evil Soul Ties
12. Spiritual Warfare

WHAT TO DO WHEN UNDER ATTACK

The methods below were extracted from the 16th Century book the ***Malleus Maleficarum*** (Hammer of Witches), written by a German Roman Catholic Priest. It supposedly reveals proven methods by which people can stop the attack of a sex demon.

5 Ways to Stop the Attacks of an Incubus Demon

1. **Exorcism:** Having a priest perform an exorcism is historically the best-known method of overcoming the attacks of the *Incubus Demon*. Unfortunately, *Incubus demons* do not obey exorcists, at least not for long. They always return.

2. **Confessions**. Exposing the activities of an incubus demon or succubus demon in your life through confessions in a church or with a priest can check any manner of spiritual warfare against you.

3. **Making the Sign of the Cross and, or Saying a Hail Mary**: A lot of people, particularly Catholics, believe in this form of deliverance. Making the sign of the cross over one's body and repeating the Hail Mary. This is another opinion that does not work.

4. **Switching Locations**. When under the attacks of an *Incubus demon*, simply moving from that location where the attack takes place to another area could be helpful. However, this is not always the case.

5. Excommunication: Excommunicating an *Incubus Demon* or a *Succubus Demon* is a process that's somewhat similar to an exorcism. In the old church, priests used this method to try to drive out these sex demons from a possessed person's body. This is another process that does not work.

That the Catholic church jailed the German priest who authored this book centuries ago, perhaps, tells a lot about the authenticity of the ideas within. A lot of priests who tested these methods on actual cases of Incubus attacks later declared them useless! In other words, they don't really work against sex demons.

So What Does Work? How Does One Get Deliverance From the Incubus Demon? How do we get rid of it ourselves?

Getting Rid of The Incubus Demon

The complex spiritual and physical methods required to get rid of the *Incubus demon* is discussed in detail in the book *Total Deliverance From Spirit Husband and Spirit Wife*.

TRUE STORIES OF INCUBUS ATTACKS

Stort Story 1.

... Okay, so last night, I had a pretty bizarre, meandering dream. The part that really stands out to me was I was in a dark place and there was some kind of ritual going on. These two people threw me down into a coffin that was in an open grave and then something had me by the waist and raped me. I actually woke up having an orgasm. While drifting back to sleep, I kept hearing this voice saying

63

things like 'I've loved you from afar for so long, I adore you, just let me love you please.'. It was a male voice, and he said it over and over and over again, just begging me. I kept getting flooded with warm and fuzzy, lovey-dovey images.

While this was happening, I heard another voice say, 'don't fall for it. It will use whatever means it can think of to try and get you to consent. It will lie to you, it will guilt you, it will imitate past lovers to get to you. Just tell it to go away'. So with a great deal of struggle, I was able to tell it to go away.

So strange. I'm not sure what brought this on, but last night, there was a storm, and our power went out. Everything in the house felt really strange and unsettling for a little while. I'm used to storms where I live but there was something sketchy going on last night for sure. Anyway, what are your thoughts? Is it something I should be concerned about returning? Should I do something like burn Sage or make a Sigil for protection? This is kind of out of the left field for me so I don't really know where to begin.

— Posted by Reddit user zombiethoven.

Short Story 2

Here is another fascinating story.

"Basically, I was going on about 5 months without getting laid, and no matter what I did, I just couldn't seem to make it happen and I was kind of obsessing over it. One night, being weird, I was lying in bed just staring into silent darkness to trip myself out. The air kind of looked static, and I thought to myself, "Just let it happen," and that when I completely relaxed and

tried to lose myself in the darkness.

I felt really comfortable and started feeling and getting rushes of new energy. It felt good. Then it went to my dick and felt super good. I was just chilling, thinking I was tripping. I felt an essence reach through my body and lightly holding onto my colon. It was gentle but it felt very strong and I felt comfortable that I wouldn't be harmed because if it wanted to harm me, it could very easily. I could feel this energy on top of me and through me.

It kept getting more intense and I loved it. I wanted more and more. That's when it hit me. "Holy shit. Is this a succubus?" I tried to lift my arms and couldn't. I felt this weighted heavy comfort mixed with sexual invigoration and I didn't even have to move. I eventually was able to lift my arm. Then I laid it down again and the process started back. I kept going back and forth because, 1. It felt awesome, and 2. From what I know, had read, about Succubi, they are energy vampires and I can't have that.

So with all the willpower I could muster, I

stopped this amazing (feeling) momentarily and forced myself out of bed to the couch where I watched YouTube videos. The sensations started again and I was super turned on. I went back and forth once again until eventually, I resorted to saying, "No. In the name of Jesus Christ, I command you to leave" (even though I'm not a Christian. I've just heard that's what you're supposed to say). I sat up for 2 hours until finally going back to sleep."
— Posted by an anonymous **user on Reddit.**

These stories and narrations of true-life encounters with the *Incubus demo*n are not only on **Reddit** but other places too. You can find a collection of them in my book, *19 True Incubus Stort Stories*.

In another book, the first book of my deliverance series, *Total Deliverance From Spirit Husband And Spirit Wife*, you'll also find a collection of over ***100 special prayers*** that are better than the one used in the last story to stop the attack of the *Incubus Demon*.

CONCLUSION

People have known about the activities of the *Incubus demon* for thousands of years. The Christian church started getting reports of it about 1500 years ago!

In many traditions and cultures, the *Incubus demon* has been used to explain away real rapes or sexual assaults where the female victims cannot talk about it openly. On the other hand, in medical science, sleep paralysis is used to explain away the activities of the *Incubus and Succubus demon.*

These vile creatures really exist, and there's quite a lot we can do to stop or prevent their attacks in our lives.

This book is merely a summary of another book that presents all the facts and information you require, including solutions to the problems brought on by Incubus demon attacks.

Rev. Ezekiel King

<u>**Total Deliverance From Spirit Husband and Spirit Wife:** *Be Free from Spirit Spouses, Marine Spirits, Incubus and Succubus Demons, and All Sex Demons*</u>

This is a book that places the power to be free in your hands. You can find it on Amazon.

THE END

Thank you for reading. If you found this book helpful, do take a minute to leave a review on it at your favorite bookstore.

May God bless and protect you.

Amen!

Ezekiel King (Revd.)
Author

OTHER BOOKS BY THE AUTHOR

Get more books by this author

- **Total Deliverance from Spirit Husband and Spirit Wife, Incubus and Succubus Demons:** *Incubus Demon and All Sex Demons of the Night*

- **Unmasking and Defeating Demons:** *150 Questions and Answers About Demons and Evil Spirits (Demon Attack, Spiritual Warfare, Demonic Possession, Demonic Covenants and Curses, Demonic Deliverance)*

- **How to Pray to God and Always Be Heard:** *The Power of Prayers Done Right*

- **19 True Incubus Short Stories:** *Incubus and Succubus True Stories, Spirit Husband and Spirit Wife Stories, Marine Spirit Spouses Stories, Ghost Sex Demons Stories – The Reality*

- **Spiritual Marriage, Women, Pregnancy, And Childbirth:** *Physical and Spiritual Warfare Against Spiritual Husband, Incubus Demon and Marine Spirits (All Sex Demons)*

Visit our website:

www.christianvy.com

Rev. Ezekiel King

ABOUT THE AUTHOR

Rev. Ezekiel King is a former co-founder of *The Holy Ghost Prayer and Healing Ministry* (1994-99). He is currently a humble worker of Christ Holy Church International.

Taking God's word and the truth of life to the people of all nations is his goal.

NOTES

77